Votive
Poems and Oracle

Votive
Poems and Oracle

by Karen Joan Kohoutek

Skull and Book Press, 2014

ISBN: 978-0-578-15022-2

Skull and Book Press, Fargo, North Dakota 58103

1

A ball of time runs from winter to winter, midnight to midnight,
away from the clock-face liturgy.

The unnameable objects are old as the world.
Biography sits in the flare, and flinches.

The cars don't know what to do at the lights,
but the soothsayer sees through the calendar.

Each fact has a dream in its fingerbones.

2

I talk a black streak.

I bite my tongue by sliding it across the sanded serrate of my
favorite tooth.
The thoughts scratch my brain.

Green and pickled and sour,
the words lie numb under the under-nub of tongue.

3

Angels sing in the aevum under the sink,
their languor stifled by white cinnamon, cocaine rearranged on
the plate.

The carpet smells of old orange peel in the corner of the kitchen,
a soft spot on the floor like the side of a pear.

Salt encrusts the saucepan, balanced tedious on the radiator.
The past's a place vast on the tip of my tongue.

4

The lights on are incongruous.
Night runs in a current through the wide banks of empty street.

A single branch strains over the snow, in a swathe of starlight.
The wind blows across the outstretched neck of every tree.

Yellow wine in rich blue glass, vinegar pink in olive-light.
The tempest's only temporary.

5

Air presses a wet rag against my skullbone.
The trunk is chewed off the tree.

Trodden with flu, I dream myself a whale vomiting tentacles, torn
from giant squid.
They squirm between my lips, round rubber squeegees, flailing
rubber flesh.

What I swallowed in the depths is wider than my insides.
What I gulped down is garbled in gobbling.

The dirty blue light hurts my lungs.
The pipe moves up and down my throat, the parts disconnected.

I smell infectious.
The virus tries to learn my language.

6

Paper blinks at the pen. The soundtrack skips at the strangest
moment.
I dream in a hard medicinal sleep.

Salt sticks to the tips of my eyelashes.
Wax fizzes on the end of the stalk.

The cold skull stares with plastic sockets from the stainless shelf.
The daughter goes flat in the glass.

In the triptych of window, a power line shakes its fist at the tree.
The curtains can't billow; they're glued to the wall.

I don't remember the persona, but it pops in as easily as a
cassette.
The first clang of sound brings it back from wherever I come
from.

I stomp upon the cast-iron stage.
The black surface scrapes off on my feet.

For a moment in the mirror, the ribbon falling flat on my arm
looks like a beetle, a leech.
The pain is in the tape deck and not in my flesh.

8

First I light the sugar on fire,
a blue flame in an antique spoon.

A dragon in the mirror brushes my teeth.
I can't taste the difference between the herb and the sugar.

The inside of my mouth curls.
My hand envies my tongue.

The blue marble tabletop has faint red veins.
Tulips stretch their heron necks, deranged.

9

I pull back the quilted blanket and find a bed of nails beneath it.
Roots hang from the ceiling onto my head.

Candles burn off the pictures of what they represent.
A mask lies empty on the table, the shell of a fruit, bereft of
something to hide.

The train shakes my body, its bones in my thighs.
I could be Pandora's twin sister, but I have no allusions.

10

The bathtub's lip is duct-taped shut,
one eye of screwed-in bolt above its gag.

In the minty pool, its sides smudged with oil,
I am gargoyle-toed, all maid and no mer.

Thick water is spiced with my blood.
The drip in the sink is amphibious, licking its lips.

It's cold walking back from the DMV,
the frontage road to another town, the K-Mart where the cop was
shot.

The metal latches of metal doors grip the street,
vaults underfoot in a cement of salt and vinegar.

A square pane of lavender breaks a wall of gnarled black brick,
the shrubs crushed into lacy balls.

12

Lipstick red fades the fastest on the posters.
Scars line both sides of the sky.

Construction-paper blue fades to bullet grey,
with vivid circles like a coaster set upon it.

We pick each other out of a crowd, from the cave of arcades,
the flare the neon leaves on eyeballs.

Am I a metaphor or am I real girl?
Am I just a layer of paper?

13

The drink glitters as if sprinkled with crushed butterflies.

At the Oriental lodge, the red plumed lamps hang bronze.
We drink sheer noodles in buttery yellowy cream.

Steam hits the powder and churns into new steam.
I scrape the bottom of my heart.

14

How far could I walk down the highway before my eyes gave
out?
The ice is suddenly no thicker than my nail.

A dining room table is strapped to the trunk like a dead deer.
The weeds drizzle out by the clank of chain link.

My brain sinks out of my skull, settles hard in my chest.
I need the words to turn the windmill.

15

The Virgin Mary emerges from a bar of soap.
It melts around her shoulders in a soft wet veil.

As it withers, the wizened mottle becomes a grotto archway.
The bar bends back; she steps through, stretches forward, rubs
her eyes.

My mouth tingles from the chemicals on my head.
A serious girl in a lab coat applies paste to my head with a
paintbrush.

My scalp turns dark flame-red.
At the temples it clumps in purple grape smudges.

My skull bends back with its wet, heavy weight.

16

The moon fades in and out but has no weakness.
For years I watched two free falls of light trickle down the
courthouse wall.

As if the bulbs are drains,
leaving water-darkened stains where the light flows and goes dry.

There's so much ruined laundry.
Fire escapes fall off the sides of hotels, and no one will sweep
them away.

It's spring in the back yard and winter out the front window.
The weatherman tips his hand back and forth, noncommittal.

17

A dryer-cloud spouts from the house next door.
A little window is singed in the wall.

The moon sits left behind in the afternoon sky.

The peonies burst into pomegranates.
A dead pigeon bares its throat, an oil-slick shimmer of feather.

Left to my own advices, I lost the dictionary for the meaning I
created.
The recording is so bad I can't hear the purr for the hiss.

18

I walk in a garden of charcoal,
ready to crush myself underfoot.

A dream of scenic hell brought me to an ugly paradise.
The insomniac looks like a maniac.

I have lost my loss,
confused the epithelium with the epithalamion.

I grow green with the thought of destruction,
a slate clean without having to wash it.

19

A fountain of night sprays around me.
Silkworms spit out my shirt.

This much rain can pull trees wider than me from the ground,
in a roar of crystal, a crash of chandelier.

A plastic stake names the flower "Cocktail Vodka Begonia."
In the octagon of earth, a lump of gum hardens into a seed, the
seed to a Buddha.

20

A dry fog like a scarf of cobwebs hangs in the upper half of the
room.
The roses fade to crumble in a pot of melodrama.

I'm down to the hotel sample shampoo,
a clogged plastic crescent of clear gelatin.

My dresses are all in shreds;
rice-size beads fall off the hems.

All that's left is the wad of dirty jeans.
The old towels smell of hazelnut.

A porcelain cup bakes on the windowsill,
the grounds fermenting, forgotten.

The boils on my face aren't a sign of the plague.
The moon grows old, sucking its cheeks in.

My existence is an arrow to a cup of coffee.
Burnt smells rise from it, the aspirin aftertaste of nondairy
creamer.

The music cracks against the bounds;
it flails, it nails my wrists down, convulsion of possession.

22

The night is a dream of good luck.
Is it a coincidence that we learn to breath?

Nothing is permanent on my skin but cat-scar,
a nick from a broken bottle, a vaccination dime.

The brush's bristles spout from seashell.
My hair has sprung a leak.

Grounds scatter into the measuring cup, turned to wax and fixed
in the sink.
My heart wants for nothing.

23

I can't blame the moon for anything that happened.

The strip mall: the concrete is a coral reef.
Walls jagged, simulated cave-rough rock.

Windshield glass lies in aquarium pebbles on the lot.
Sky itches for the scratchy fingers of the trees.

The clouds are darkest closest to the yellow,
and pale toward invisible stars.

24

In the pillars, the smooth white grooves dig in switchblade-deep.
My palm is the x-ray of a hand.

An enlarged thumbprint of muddy boot swirls dark and wet on
the floor.
The drop of ink could be a speck of blood.

The ceramic apple is candy-glazed with dust.
The tile is a little square of memory, but I don't know whose.

25

Onstage, good luck is bad luck.
The word "blessing" curdles in my throat.

The cat stares out of intangible eyes.
Her fingertips are pinpricks.

Silver erodes next to my skin.
Love drips from the hole in the hose of my heart.

The saints burn candles for me.
I never thought I'd come to this conclusion.

26

A string of UFOs hangs over the folding doors,
b.b. pockmarks on the vinyl seats.

A fringe of white scarf trails on the silver surface,
ketchup-flecked and soda-spotted.

A fleet of sirens comes down with the rain.
Coffee spills in a brown vein down my arm.

Thunder slams like a truck into my dream,
a countdown from the lightning.

I don't have a season to shed my skin.
Our selves are the doppelgangers of our cells.

If the hand of god reached down to me,
my place is in the vat of salt.

The sidewalk is blown sideways.
It's a betrayal to long for the level.

28

The seashells are tiny as baby fingernails.
Doomed birds flutter in the smothered pines.

I don't want to know what makes the lake silver and the river red.
I know I would misuse the weather.

Leaves crawl along the trees. The ground shudders under their
shaking.
Night scorches the dark onto the earth.

The camera points away from me.
I don't recommend my face.

The only light in a stranger's kitchen is the red point on the coffee machine.
The tips of roofs are a row of birdhouses.

A paperback hunches creased on the couch.
A smell of paint comes off the pages.

Fluorescent light hangs stretched in a cage above the table.
One shadow crowds another out.

The liquid stains my teeth to the bone.

30

The sun's calming warm slowly turns to pressure,
like a kind word grown increasingly heavy.

The door drags and scrapes at the floor,
limping against the threshold.

The bitter dry blossoms and I spit the weeds out of my mouth,
a mockery of a hot summer day.

Some people love the ocean to drowning.
I bake my own coffee, I roast my own milk.

31

The bus is chance made metal.
It drives with a bag over its head, covered in a mesh of ads.

The parking lot is an orange dessert in a flat pan.
The magnets in the sidewalk grasp at my feet.

An asteroid green masquerades as the horizon.
The flag flap sounds like footsteps. The interstate never lets up.

32

I didn't write the hoax.
I scratch over the revelation.

Words fall on my head like stones on the roof,
a crack on my tongue, smoke in my palms.

Divinity cleans up after the devil.
When I write my bible, heaven will flood the bathroom floor.

33

Stems blossom from the red soil of sloshing liquid,
in a glass glossy red and green with enamel tulips.

Wine blackberries my tongue.
Salt strips scales and flecks of flesh from the cave of my mouth.

My foot turns in a rickety shoe.
No one gets the world, but I dream of eating the night.

34

The skating rink is blank and out of season.
A rich smell from the river, vegetable soup.

The wind blows hot and the grass bristles, hostile.
Green has become a glare, pitted with tiny blue weeds.

It's never safe to say anything.
I will close my peripheral eye.

35

The sun wobbles unstable then steadies itself.
The earth's at its disposal.

Outside the day is a circle of green.
Albino dust bleaches the brown air.

The church is espaliered, elongated vine on black slick stone,
its shadows full of repine.

A small clay man stands in the garden,
a scarlet flower grown in front of his mouth, a microphone.

The water in the swimming pool lies awake all night.

36

Sugar gets in the way of everything: sugar, salt, milk, and coal.
Incense, pine, snakes smoke up the spine of the cold candle.

Wax turns to wet, then solders back together.

The King James Bible is the big book of voodoo,
a fortress of mortar and epistle.

My church doesn't have holy water, but they pour something on
the babies.
There were extinguishing circumstances.

The white paper skeleton holds the brown one in its arms,
skull upon shoulder blade.

I live in the dream mercado.

The hollow stores are open all night,
gauze-built stages soaked and stiffened with merlot.

I walk backstage, stiff in an Ophelia dress, hair halfway long and shorn.
The pearls are fake but the diamonds are real.

38

The gravel chickenscratch of yard has been chewed down by
tires.
The garden is tart with the taste of perfect dirt.

Crows bark in the trees.
Clouds reach their hands almost down to the trees' green crowns.

The garbage sits quiet and hooded beside the garage.
Pigeons who've lost their religion wander mournful on the
sidewalk.

We drove down to the fake lake, pottery mud, gravel worn to ash,
a tower of volcanic crag under the noon.

The rocks grow thicker, twisted,
purple spine on mother of pearl.

Trees spindle, growing thin and dry under the canary leaves,
oval and diamond-shaped.

The dirt road sits a furrow in the earth.
No tide ever comes in, just a perpetual lapping of time.

40

The clatter of pot and pan is the muffle of mutter and curse.

Ink overwhelms the idea, and sound eats up the image.
I'm not on the roof and I'm not in the basement, and I'm not
awake.

The sky is a square of black.
A moth sticks on the glass like a piece of Scotch tape.

The muse hangs dusty on the wall, hunched on the globe.
She's in her own little world.

41

The limes are darker than lime green.
The word "vanity" is the first thing I see.

The fast flutter of train shudders the house.
Flashing lights cut fine lines, a grid along my eyeballs.

The summer street is meshed orange.
Fattened pythons of root burrow through the earth.

42

I dream up a fear of a straight road, a highway cut through earth.
The house has turrets. The yard has bats the shuttered arch gave
birth to.

Wind begins to whistle sideways through its teeth.
The ripples make a thumbprint on the river.

There's nothing wrong with our bones.
They're slim and easy to swallow.

43

The bike looks wrought-iron sunk into the rack.
The tower spokes torture the sky.

A box-worth of vines, stone-encrusted, protrude from the side of
the church.
A flat plaque on the door announces the God.

The same trees still lean. Lanky branches leak out of their bodies.
The blue's spread so thin I can almost see through the sky.

It's too late to carve my name in the sidewalk.
Duct tape holds it together.

Crisp wedding rain gallops over green earth,
falls straight into silvery threads.

It burns rivulets on the window.
The powerline glistens, ropy with wet.

I burn impatient. The sound turns me drunk.
The wind blows down my throat. The stars escape the sky.

44

I always hope the missing choose to disappear.

A cranky language is thorny in my mouth.
It's easy to choose the elusive.

Paradise doesn't make anybody happy.
In the graveyard, the ankhs are anchored to the ground.

45

An elephant sleeps at the base of my skull,
carved on a leather oval, stick spearing a bun of hair.

Parrot-colored paper rustles in the box.
Wine decays sweet in the glass.

Empty vinyl arms flop over the side of the chair.
My boots track crushed autumn onto the floor.

46

I wanted a stone cavern of a room, carved with light, shelves
inside and ivy out.
White tea, green tea, every tea but blue.

This is the dream forced down my throat.
Close one eye and then the other and watch the objects jump
through space.

I gave away my soul singled and crumpled,
and got it back the same way.

No difference in the amount of dirt.
My bones still rise to the surface.

Barbed shrubs line the suburbs.
A thick bandage of frame straps the windows to the walls.

We walk among the clawed crowd.
Pearl creeps up and down the bannister among the oak festoon.

Wooden railings imprison the pumpkins.
A jet leaves a scratch against the sky.

Rain turns the traffic into a funeral procession.
Pale pink light settles on a dirty street.

I write "diewalk" for "sidewalk."

48

The coffeepot gurgles in its wide throat.
The radio begins to boil. I step around a grocery bag full of
stylized skulls.

On tv, the sun hasn't come up yet.
The toaster holds the bread in its coal-warm hands and blows on
it.

Sparrows pick over the tombstones of garbage cans.
It's a long-winded siren. All is pristine at the end of the block.

49

Everything washes away on our street.
In the brownstone bay window, the window has no bay.

Right now the ugly street still unscrolls,
block letters full of hideous bargains.

It's trick or treat in the garden, full of lamp and birch.
The open sky hangs over us, a random light full of feist.

The neon noodle bowl sticks to the side of the bank.

50

The morning surfaces, light floating to the top of the earth.
Night sinks over it, gravity down to the core.

A wall of bone crusts over the sky.
The barrier of buildings can't fend off the air.

Somewhere out there, or somewhere in here,
the darkness is another character.

51

In the smudged sky, dark grey scrapes over dark blue,
thick and clumped frosting spread with an oval-edged butter
knife.

On all sides there's a deep drop into blackness.
Below is a bionic landscape, highway and bead of light.

I am soaked in the dream.
The night makes promises but I can't remember them.

52

In my favorite November, the streets had crooked sidewalks.

The one-way by the cemetery, the blue-tint trees around the
graves,
water up past their knees.

I glimpsed the pedestal, the sandstone idol on top of the
tombstone.
The moon hesitated at the crossroad.

He said, no one cares if you've been in the house,
stood in the door where the murderer stood.

The trees move of their own will, regardless of the wind.
North air entombs them in a line by the river.

The ruffle in the pheasant's neck spits in the bushes like a deck
shuffling.
Trees jut into the sunset, stonehenge-edged.

Thick frosting froth floats on the cocoa river.
The soil smells rusty tin.

54

There isn't enough noise to wake the dead.
I always feel protective.

A plaque of rules at the cemetery keeps the souls in line.
No statues, no shrubs, no glass jars.

The Lord of the Cemetery is supposed to work the mal.
But how can the graveyard be evil?

There are too many crossroads to leave offerings.
We pronounce it "Sadder Day."

55

I dip into the vat of air, the first true cold.
My body flinches from the remembered blow.

The night air slides a thin piece of ice into the antiseptic lung.
Cold slinks around the bones, the bones stick to the skin.

I don't need to pick up stray luck anymore.
I leave the pennies where they lie.

The sky and the ground flip places.
The shelter keeps nothing out.

56

This moment the line cuts down my face.
Half of me is shadow, the half inside my body.

There's so much water and sulfur in hell,
and we don't know what's in heaven.

I can't do and I can't undo.
You don't want to crack open the egg in my chest.

57

The candle glass is cold in the window sill,
two El Nino Fidencios, one painted in black suit and tie, one
blue.

A far-away galaxy dribbles through space.
The sky slowly lowers until it touches the ground.

My eyes slide off the buttered surface of the page.
Trying to think is chewing on coal, breathing a bubble of mud.

58

The sofa comes in a box like a coffin.
I pick up the taper and break the candle's back.

The radiator fizzes in the corner.
A scrappy scroll of calendar furls on the wall.

Aluminum shelves hang in rows like butcher knives in notches,
shotguns lined against the window of the cab.

Birds leave feathery footprints in the snow, thin and leafy.
Melting and freezing, ice turns to waxy sludge.

Winter has nothing like lightning.
The violence is muffled by snow.

Like it or not, all angels have wings.
Some people tear them off when they see them.

Even King Lear knew that.

The portents begin to seem unimportant.
The sky burns aquarium green, destined to be clandestine.

60

The cat is tabbied by shadow.
Is the sky faking that multicolored moon?

The blue-palmed portrait of your hand is studded with jewels on
the wrists,
a nerve string of fingers.

The lifeline in my hand is strong, but it's only ink.
Puddles and netting indigo the grooves.

The phrenology mask hides the enlightenment,
ideas fused to my porcelain head.

61

The room swelters with the memory of every room.
At every angle there's a fracture toward the past.

Black vistas spread through space, black slippery spaces.
The air pulls away from us. It's full of lace.

The hostesses are brittle as the bone china saucers,
their houses gone, their furniture polished.

My skin will fade, dead leaves crushing and sinking to soil.
I'll be forgotten before anyone else.

62

The windows fuzz with wet moss.
The long glass melts but not the lucky wax.

The candle huddles like a jello dessert,
every stripe a different flavor.

Pocked with multicolored air,
it jiggles when it burns, floats in its glass corset.

Vicious yellow eyes glow out of the morning,
sulfurous streetlights leftover from night.

63

I don't have fifty nouns total,
or seven days to burn them in.

On the egg-white snow, egg-yellow dog piss.
My shoes leave heart-shaped foot-prints.

The wire is cold in my lobes.
The stars retreat. Gallons of sky in between us.

64

The shower curtain glows unholy.
Dark seeps from a circle of thorn, a boiling bulb of light.

The medicine cabinet swings open in a glare of glitter,
and flattens again, serene mirror.

My eyes are still in the sockets.

65

In a cab, you pay for every stoplight.
Each car has a pair of eyes, wobbling red.

Compressed, the tree grows into a fern.
Garbage Can Bob writes his name on the wall.

We are victims of the angle of the earth.
I throw thoughts away on the surface.

The stairs protrude in metal buck teeth,
the brick wall turns mossy soft.

There's no end to the swallowing.
The flippant heart still breaks.

66

There are fangs in my mouth with nothing to bite,
but this pen has a hair-trigger.

My hand's shadow is a beak on the page,
claws to catch my own finger.

I've lived just long enough
to begin to learn a language.

How to Use the Oracle

This book is designed so that you can cut out the (mostly) couplets and (occasional) single lines from the poems, mix them up, and pull slips at random, to create your own poems or individualized fortunes. Use as many lines as you want.

If you don't want to cut lines out of the book, you can use the oracle this way: take a couple of regular six-sided dice. Roll one of them one time.

If you roll a 1, then take both dice and roll them, to get a number from 2 to 12. That's the number of your poem.

If you roll a 6, then roll one die one time, and add a zero to that number. So if you roll a 1, it's poem 10; if you roll a 2, it's poem 20, and so on.

If you roll a 2, 3, 4, or 5, then just roll both dice to get the number of a poem. If the lefter of the dice in the roll is a 3, and the righter is a 6, then it's poem 36. Or you could roll one die twice, to get the first and second digits.

If you use the dice method, then the blank space on each page is available for your notes and impressions.

Once you find your fortune, many of you will immediately wonder what it means. Like an oracle, a poem both means and transcends meaning. When you live with the words and the symbols and the dreams, eventually it begins to make sense to you. Or if it doesn't, it will spark a peculiar symbol of your own, a pair of words that would never go together, but will fall in love when they meet.

If you need more explanation, go outside in a quiet place and stand under the moon. If you can see it, look at it. Think about the words, and other words of your own, words for beautiful things. That's your fortune. Enjoy it.

Acknowledgements

Votive 16 appeared on the website 42opus, in a slightly different form.

About the Author

Karen Joan Kohoutek grew up in Wadena, Minnesota, and now lives in Fargo, North Dakota, where she is known for her annual library program, Ghost Stories for Grown-Ups. In 2002, she received a Master of Fine Arts in Creative Writing from Minnesota State University Moorhead. These are not the poems she submitted for her thesis. Her previous book, *The Jack-o-Lantern Box*, is available through Lulu and Smashwords.

You can visit her online at octoberzine.blogspot.com, or contact her at octoberzine@gmail.com.

Photo credit: Christopher A. Smith

christopherasmith58102@gmail.com
christopherasmith58102.tumblr.com